Silverton School Library
1160 Snowden
Box 128
Silverton, CO 81433

D0971587

APRIL FOOLS' DAY

APRIL FOOLS' DAY

by Emily Kelley

pictures by C.A. Nobens

Carolrhoda Books · Minneapolis

Copyright © 1983 by CAROLRHODA BOOKS, INC.
All rights reserved. International copyright secured.
No part of this book may be reproduced in any form whatsoever
without permission in writing from the publisher except for
the inclusion of brief quotations in an acknowledged review.
Manufactured in the United States of America

LIBRARY OF CONGRESS CATALOGING IN PUBLICATION DATA

Kelley, Emily.
  April Fools' Day.

  (A Carolrhoda on my own book)
  Summary: Explains the customs and traditions
connected with the merry pranks of April fooling, and
provides several versions of how April Fools' Day came
about.
  1. April Fools' Day—Juvenile literature.
[1. April Fools' Day] I. Nobens, C. A., ill.
II. Title. III. Series.
GT4995.A6K44   1983   394.2′683   82-23559
ISBN 0-87614-218-8 (lib. bdg.)

      5   6   7   8   9   10   92   91   90   89   88

for Christopher

This is going to be the worst book
you have ever read!
It is boring,
and the pictures are ugly.
You might as well
put it down right now.

Wait a minute....
April Fool!

Have you ever been fooled
on the first day of April?

You're not the only one.

April 1 has been a day for fooling

for hundreds of years.

It's not an official holiday

like Thanksgiving,

but it is celebrated every year

in the United States, Great Britain,

Canada, Australia, and France.

No one is sure exactly when

April fooling began.

Some people believe that it started

in Roman times—over 2,000 years ago.

They think it began

with the Roman story of Proserpina.

Proserpina's mother was named Ceres.

Ceres was a goddess.

She ruled over grain and the harvest.

One day Proserpina was picking flowers.

Pluto, the god of the dead, saw her.

He thought she was beautiful.

He wanted to make her his queen.

Pluto decided to steal Proserpina.
He carried her away
to the land of the dead.
Proserpina did not want to go with him.
She did not want to live
in the land of the dead.

Ceres heard Proserpina's cries for help.

She began to look for her daughter,

but her search was only a "fool's errand."

Ceres was only chasing after

the echo of Proserpina's voice.

She could not go

to the land of the dead.

No one except Pluto

could go back and forth

between the land of the living

and the land of the dead.

Today some people say

that April fooling started

with the story of how Pluto fooled Ceres.

Another legend
of how April Fools' Day began
is the story of "The Wise Men of Gotham."
King John was the king of England
during the 1200s.
One spring day
he was on his way to Nottingham.
He was planning to walk
through the meadow of Gotham.
There was a custom in those days
that any ground the king walked on
became a public road.
The people of Gotham did not want
their meadow to become a road.
They kept King John out of it.

Of course the king was very angry.

Later he sent an officer

to find out why

the people had been so rude.

He wanted to punish them.

The people heard

that an officer was coming.

They gathered together

to decide what to do about it.

This is what the king's officer found

when he got to Gotham.

Some people were trying
to drown a fish in a pond.

Others were dragging their wagons
to the tops of their barns.
They said they wanted
to shade the roofs from the sun.

Still others were rolling cheese
down a hill.
They said it would find its way
to the Nottingham market.

When the king's officer saw all this,

he thought they were all fools.

He told King John

not to bother punishing them.

And that, say some,

is how April Fools' Day began.

Still another popular belief
is that April Fools' Day began in France.
In 1564 King Charles IX decided to use
the new Gregorian calendar.
This calendar changed
the first day of the year
from April 1 to January 1.
Now news traveled slowly in those days.
Some people didn't find out
about the change right away.
Others simply didn't want
the first day of the year to change.

These people kept right on
with the old customs for the new year.
They visited friends
and gave presents to one another,
but they were celebrating
on the wrong day!
Other people began to play jokes
on those who still celebrated
the new year on April 1.
Eventually this April fooling
became a custom in France.

Here is yet another story

of how April Fools' Day began.

Some people in France noticed

that in the spring

there were many more fish in the streams.

That was because all the young fish

had just hatched.

These young fish were simple to catch.

They were easily fooled by a hook.

Soon French *people* who were easily fooled

were called "poisson d'Avril"

(pwah-SONE dah-VREEL).

That means April fish.

April fooling became
very popular in France.
Soon no one wanted to start
anything important on April 1.

People were afraid of being fooled.

But that didn't stop Napoleon Bonaparte.

He married his second wife on April 1,

and he was nicknamed "poisson d'Avril."

April fooling became popular in Britain
early in the 1700s.

One popular trick in Scotland
was to send people on foolish errands.

Some poor person might be tricked
into looking for hens' teeth
or pigeons' milk.

Hens don't have teeth,
and pigeons don't give milk!

Another popular prank in Scotland
was called "hunting the gowk."
A gowk is a cuckoo bird.
Let's go back 250 years
and see how this worked.

It is the morning of April 1, 1737.

Mr. Andrews gives a letter

to Walter Young.

"Please deliver this letter to Mr. Scott

on Dundee Lane," he tells Walter.

"But that is way out on the edge
of town," Walter says.

"I know it is far away,"
says Mr. Andrews,
"but this is an important letter.
I need a loan, and Mr. Scott
is a very rich man."
So Walter starts on his way
to Dundee Lane.
By the time he gets there,
he is tired and hungry,
but he delivers the important letter.

Mr. Scott reads the message.

"Oh, I'm sorry," he says.

"I cannot loan the money to Mr. Andrews,
but Mr. Blackburn will be able to.

He lives another mile down the road.

Please take the letter to him."

So the poor messenger
begins walking again.

Inside the letter
the real message said,

"This is the first of April.

Hunt the gowk another mile."

Walter can't find another house
on Dundee Lane.
Finally he returns to town.
There he finds his fellow townsmen

waiting for him to come back.

They are all laughing.

Of course they think it is great fun,

but Walter is not so sure!

Many people in London
were fooled in 1857.
In those days there was a zoo
in the Tower of London.
Once a year
the lions in the zoo were washed.
Everyone wanted to see that.
On April 1, 1857,
hundreds of people bought tickets.
But when they got to the Tower of London,
they found they were all April fools.
A prankster playing an April fool joke
had sold them fake tickets.

April fooling came to the New World
with the early English settlers.
Many of the jokes
were played by children.
One favorite joke
was to put a sign that said
"Kick Me" or "Pinch Me"
on someone's back.
The person wearing the sign
was very confused,
but the person playing the joke
had fun watching.

Another trick

was to cover pieces of cotton

with melted chocolate.

Many people were fooled

by this "cotton candy."

Some people liked to put salt

in the sugar bowl.

Others put sugar in the salt shaker.

One joke that became popular

in the United States went like this.

Someone would tie a string to a purse,

then leave the purse on the sidewalk.

Then he or she would hide,

holding the other end of the string.
Soon someone else would bend over
to pick up the purse,
but suddenly the purse
was snatched away.

This joke became very well known.

One year there was an old purse

lying on the sidewalk,

but no one would pick it up.

No one wanted to be an April fool.

Finally a brave little boy

did pick it up.

Inside the purse was $80.

Someone had *really* lost her purse,

and the little boy got a reward

for returning it.

It was not an April fool joke this time.

All the April fools were the people

who wouldn't pick up the purse.

False messages have long been popular.
Once, in California,
eight senators found the same message
on their desks.
It told them to meet right away
in the governor's office.
They were all embarrassed to find
that the governor hadn't called
a meeting at all.

On April Fools' Day
some zoos get more calls for the animals
than they do for people.

In 1959 a radio disc jockey in Hawaii
created quite a stir.

Hawaii had just become a state.

The disc jockey told the people
that their taxes from the year before
would be given back to them.

Imagine what excitement this caused!

The point of April Fools' Day
is to play jokes with such fun
that the victim laughs too.
Lies and mean jokes do not count.
Merry April fooling has been going on
for many centuries.
It is still popular today,
and people will probably enjoy it
for years to come.
Many years from now
people will probably fall
for the same tricks
that we are falling for now.
And many of these are the same tricks
people fell for hundreds of years ago.

So beware next April 1.

Don't be surprised

if you find salt on your cereal

instead of sugar.

If people start pinching you,

check to see if there is a sign

on your back.

If you find a purse on the sidewalk,

will you dare to pick it up?

Just don't be surprised when *you*
are an April fool!